RESTO

GREA.

A SPIRITUAL HANDBOOK
FOR TRANSFORMING THE WORLD

DADI JANKI

£3.00 LH W52

Dedicated to Dadi Janki
in celebration of her 90th Birthday

Edited by Sharonah Stillerman

ISBN 1-886872-30-9

Published by Brahma Kumaris Information Services Ltd.
Global Co-operation House,
65 Pound Lane, London NW10 2HH UK.

© Copyright 2006 Brahma Kumaris Information Services Ltd.

This book has been compiled and edited by the Brahma
Kumaris Information Services Ltd, in association
with the Brahma Kumaris World Spiritual University (UK).
Registered Charity No. 269971.

Illustrations by Darius
Designed by BookDesign™, London
Printed by Power Digital Printing Co Ltd. Hong Kong

www.bkpublications.com
email: enquiries@bkpublications.com

www.bkwsu.org

RESTORING OUR
GREATNESS

A SPIRITUAL HANDBOOK
FOR TRANSFORMING THE WORLD

DADI JANKI

BK PUBLICATIONS

an imprint of

BRAHMA KUMARIS INFORMATION SERVICES LTD.

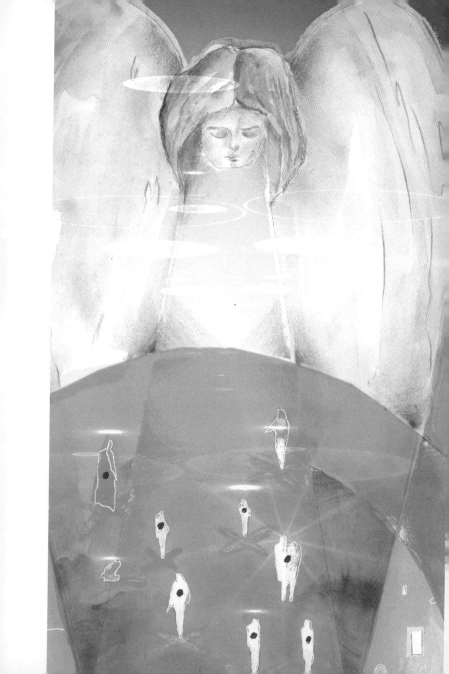

IF NOT YOU,
THEN WHO?

IF NOT NOW,
THEN WHEN?

CONTENTS

Dadi Janki

FOREWARD

Nestled in the Aravali mountains of Rajasthan, Northwest India, in a place called Mt. Abu, can be found a little piece of heaven on earth called Madhuban (its name means, 'Forest of Honey'). It is the headquarters of a unique institution, the Brahma Kumaris World Spiritual University.

Led by women, this flourishing organization, which is dedicated to creating a world of peace, health and happiness. People from around the world flock to Madhuban to experience its powerful, peaceful atmosphere and study the principles and practices on which it is based. All leave touched by the humility, love and generosity of its residents, who serve with genuine happiness and enthusiasm.[1]

Dadi Janki, (the word 'Dadi' means 'elder sister') has been with the Brahma Kumaris almost from its start in 1936.

Mentored in the early days by Brahma Baba, founder of the organization and sustained by qualities of courage, determination and love for truth, Dadi proved herself to be a natural teacher and leader.

In 1974, she came to the West to start the process of establishing the organization on a global scale. In her current role as joint administrative head of the Brahma Kumaris, she has been the inspiration for a number of visionary projects, including 'A Million Minutes of Peace' for which the organization received seven United Nations Peace Messenger Awards. Since then, Dadi has been designated a 'Wisdom Keeper' at two United Nations' conferences: 'The Earth Summit' (1992) in Brazil and 'Habitat' (1996) in Turkey.

Having travelled the world, tending to the spiritual needs of people from all walks of life, cultures and professions, Dadi Janki is well aware of the need for transformation at all levels of society. With great love, she offers clear, practical and empowering solutions to the challenges we face, based on a deep understanding of the power of goodness and its role in restoring the greatness of the human spirit.

This book contains some of the treasures she has gathered during her spiritual journey. As you read, enjoy, and apply the wisdom to be found in it, you will discover how hungry the soul is to experience its spiritual greatness.

You will become part of the rising tide of powerful, positive, spiritual energy that is working to restore harmony and balance to this wounded world.

Neville Hodgkinson

Ex-Science Correspondent, *The Sunday Times'*

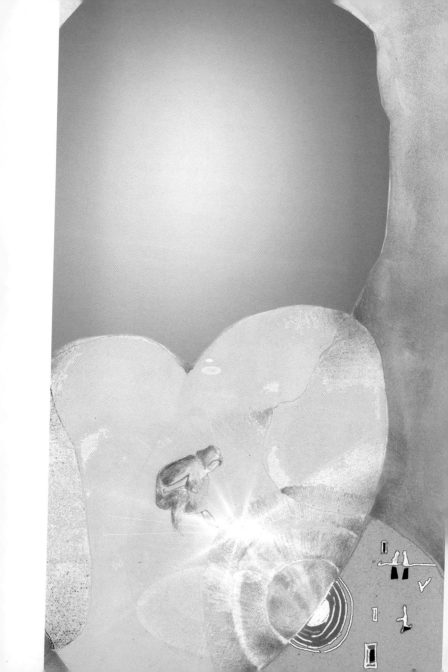

INTRODUCTION

In these troubled times, when the forces of negativity seem to be tightening their grip on the world, it can be difficult to maintain our faith in the goodness of humanity and the importance of being and doing good.

We need to remind ourselves that in many ancient civilisations, there are references to a time when the earth was like heaven – a beautiful garden, such as the gardens of Eden or Allah, in which blissful, 'god-like' beings lived in peace and harmony with themselves and nature. It was a time of innocence, when the lion and the lamb lay side by side.

Relics of that past remain. Ancient books contain descriptions of amazing arts and sciences, many buildings contain strange and beautiful carvings, or paintings of heavenly scenes and mythological stories tell of a time when gods walked the earth. Each culture has its own heroes, heroines, sacred beliefs and traditions. These suggest how great human beings have been and, perhaps, can be again.

The history of more recent times seems to be one of increasing conflict and sorrow, as the forces of greed and competition wreak havoc on the earth. Despite the efforts of the great faith traditions and people of goodwill throughout the world, things seem to be going from bad to worse. Global poverty, violence in its many forms and environmental destruction threaten to engulf us all and there is much uncertainty as to our future. What to do?

The assertion, by spiritual teachers in the past, that the challenges we face can be transformed through the help of God, has not had much effect. Exhortation and inspiration are not enough. We want practical proof that things can change, and a new strategy for creating the change we seek.

A method for personal and world transformation is clearly set out in this handbook of insights taken from Dadi Janki's talks. It is a four-step process.

Firstly, we need a clear understanding of the nature of the self – an awareness that we are all innately good, eternal, spiritual beings; beings of peace, love, purity and happiness, who have lost our spiritual power and forgotten who we are.

Secondly, there has to be accurate knowledge of God, or the Supreme Being, and His[2] role in the world. We need to reconnect with this infinite Source of goodness in order to recharge the depleted battery of the soul. This is achieved through the practice of meditation known as Brahma Kumaris Raja Yoga Meditation.

Thirdly, we change ourselves. By putting into practice the insights we gain through meditation and spiritual study, we learn new ways of thinking and being. These ways improve our self esteem and relationships with others.

Fourthly, we change the world. This is a natural consequence of the first three steps. A soul that is peaceful, happy and content will naturally share these qualities, and will want to show others the ways to achieve them.

And so, as our greatness is restored, the ripples of peace, love and light will spread and the world will be transformed.

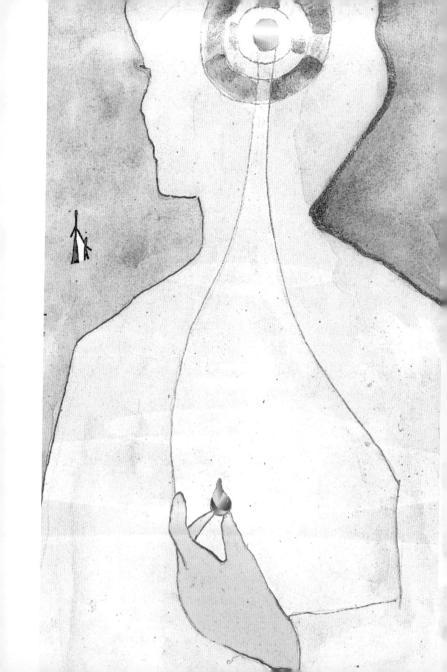

O N E

INSIDE KNOWLEDGE

The question "who are we?" is one that has preoccupied philosophers from the beginning of human history. The answer has a profound effect on the way we relate to the self, others, and the world. It becomes the foundation of our security and the base from which we operate.

So, who are we? Are we fallen gods and goddesses, or have we always been sinful souls? Are we rational beings, who just happen to exist because of some chance chemical reaction in the evolutionary process of the Earth? Are we just another species of animal, with an extra gene or two, that enable us to communicate more effectively and, therefore, rule the world?

There are so many models that contribute to our understanding of human nature and behaviour – economic, political, sociological, medical, scientific, psychological and theological. However, their competing claims for our support and attention have led to confusion and uncertainty as to the real value of human beings in the 21st century. It is as if the mirror of identity has been shattered. Each fragment gives us a glimpse of who we are, but never the overall picture.

Dadi Janki is someone who has studied the nature of the human spirit for many years, and she has no doubts about who we are. She holds up a mirror that is clean and whole, in which we can see the true self that lies beneath the other, limited perspectives.

Through her presence and philosophy, Dadi reminds us of what, deep inside, we already know – that our essential, fundamental identity is spiritual. She believes that each of us is a soul and that we each have a divine nature, a spiritual DNA, made up of five basic qualities: peace, love, happiness, purity, and power. In other words, that we are innately good.

This understanding of the self offers a profound message of hope for us all. If our original nature is one of goodness, all we have to do is act in accordance with that nature and stop doing things that go against it. We need to support and encourage each other, to tap into our goodness and allow it to flourish with love and patience. To suppress and control our loving nature through fear or force is often the way of this world. But this can only lead to sorrow and the destruction of the human spirit.

Peace is the one quality, in particular, that Dadi claims will open us up to all the others. In this chapter, she elaborates on this concept, by sharing her own realisations and experience of the spiritual self.

The Soul Is Peace

One of the most important lessons to learn about the self is contained within the expression, 'O*m Shanti*'.

'*Om Shanti*' means, 'I, the soul, am peace.'

If we use this expression in the right way, it opens us to an inner secret : we desire peace because the intrinsic quality of the soul is peace.

We never have to ask for peace.

We *are* peace.

This is the first lesson: each of us is a peaceful soul.

We need to understand this.

Try it and see. Look at the self within.

Take a moment to say, with feeling,

"I, the soul, am peace. *Om Shanti.*"

Recognise yourself.

The Soul Is Separate From Its Roles

When we say the word, 'I', we need to think deeply about exactly what that word means.

Does our name, or the name of our country, religion, or profession come to mind? Do we think, "I am a man, I am a woman. I am this many years old"?

If the answer is yes, we deceive ourselves. Such aspects are associated with the body alone. They are physical and perishable.

This makes them very different from the real 'I'.

The real 'I' is divine, a tiny point of pure light that is spiritual and unique. This light is non-physical and imperishable.

This true self sits in the body, but is not part of the body.

The peaceful soul, inside the body, is playing out many different roles. Each soul is an actor. We are not the roles we play. We are not English, or French, or American, or Japanese.

We are more than a wife, son, father, friend, engineer, teacher, or salesperson. We are more than a man, or a woman, or a child. These are only our roles.

They refer to the body, not the true self.

They are all distinct and separate from the real 'I'.

It is because we lose ourselves in our roles that our inner peace also gets lost.

We, the peaceful souls, *are*.

We always have existed; we always will.

We existed long before our body took shape, and we

will continue to exist, long after the body loses its shape.

We, peaceful souls, are eternal.

Who are you? Who am I? All of us – you and I – are souls. God's children.

It is good to think about these things, deeply.

External Influence Destroys Peace

Another reason why the peaceful soul has lost its peace is that the unhappiness of the outside world has penetrated the inner being.

How did this happen?

We lost control over our mind.

The mind, like a receiver, tunes into one experience or another. When the mind is strongly influenced by the turmoil and sorrow of the outer world, that becomes our experience.

When we give our minds over to external circumstances, they invade the self.

It is better to teach the mind to tune into the eternal peaceful soul within. The mind knows how to do this. It just needs reminding.

Tune into your inner strength and you will remain uninfluenced by external situations.

This is an important aspect of '*Om Shanti*'.

Extroversion Creates Unhappiness

Extroversion is the habit of losing oneself in one or another, aspect of the outer world.

With extroversion, the mind and physical senses race outwards, wanting to know what is going on in everyone else.

We become extroverted because we have grown accustomed to satisfying our needs and desires through our physical senses. Such satisfaction is always temporary.

In fact, most of our needs reflect a spiritual emptiness, and nothing physical can fulfil the needs of the spirit.

Yet, we continue the habit of looking outside ourselves to try and satisfy these spiritual needs. People, possessions and our own habits consistently attract and trap the mind. Even if we wish to, we find we cannot remain independent of them.

Despite knowing that it is a world of sorrow, we do not let go of it easily. We remain mentally attached.

This is the reason why many people embark on a spiritual search. There is a feeling that something within is being overlooked.

Introversion is a matter of going within, to understand and experience the self.

Recreating Peace

Who am I? This question is very sweet, once we know the answer.

The feeling of inner peace that comes from saying, "I am a peaceful soul, *Om shanti*", is just a beginning.

From peace, there will be feelings of love. From love will come feelings of happiness. Ultimately, all three lead to a feeling of personal power.

These four feelings are the basis of good meditation.

To feel them and then to carry them into our life is to make meditation practical.

It is possible to become free from tension and negativity. It is only a matter of paying attention.

Make it a practice to go deep within.

Keep trying to understand and experience the meaning of '*Om Shanti.*'

Repeatedly remind yourself of who you are. We have been so removed from this understanding that it now almost has to be 'drummed in' to our consciousness.

Refuse to let go of your peace, patience and love.

TWO

MAKING THE
CONNECTION

*Much confusion and controversy surround the existence and
nature of God and His role in the world.*

*Who is God? Does He exist? Does it really matter anyway?
These are not just academic questions. They go right to the heart of
the problems facing the world today. Different religions have
different ideas about who God is and how He should be worshipped.
These differences have caused much bloodshed over the centuries. A
legacy of religious intolerance continues to this day and threatens to
destroy the world. We need to take a fresh, objective look at who, or
what, we mean by God and go beyond the current confusion.*

God is much misunderstood. For some, He is a vengeful

being, who sends the wicked to hell for all eternity. For others, He is Love. For some, He is the equivalent of a benign old man in the sky, for others He is imageless. For some, there is only one God. For others, God is universal energy, omnipresent, even in the pebbles and stones. Or, He is a mystery, to be worshipped, feared, or abhorred, depending on your point of view.

Little wonder that including among the educated, many declare themselves atheists or agnostics when asked if they believe in God, and go in search of their own answers to the meaning of life.

Even if we want to believe in, and rely on, God, where do we start? How can we communicate with someone we don't know, who may not even exist?

There has to be an accurate understanding of who God is and a common language, if communication is to be successful.

Dadi Janki has a very clear understanding of the nature and form of God and His role in transforming the world. Through the practice of Raja Yoga meditation, as taught by the Brahma Kumaris, she has experienced God at the deepest levels and formed a close and personal relationship with Him. For Dadi, God is:

the Supreme Being, *a living soul with a divine personality, a point of light energy, similar to ourselves, but with one important difference. Unlike all other souls, the Supreme Soul* does not enter the physical world and take birth in a body and so does not lose His power. Being beyond the influence of the physical world, the Supreme Soul remains an eternal source of divine light and energy. This notion of God as a form of light is recognised, at least symbolically, by many different faith traditions;

the Father of all souls. As the children of God, we are all brothers and sisters, who belong to one spiritual family. Therefore, there is no need to fight each other;

an Ocean of Knowledge whose role at this time is to help us remember our divine origins and restore peace and harmony on earth. He does this by giving us knowledge of the meaning and purpose of life on earth, His role and ours and what we need to do to restore our original greatness and become like Him. He does not wish us to worship Him, but rather to communicate honestly with Him, access His healing powers of peace and love, through silent remembrance, and assist Him in His task of transformation.

Dadi Janki's understanding and experience of the personality of God removes, at a stroke, one of the greatest misunderstandings that prevent many people from trusting and loving God, namely, that He is a fearsome, wrathful Being who is responsible for our sorrow and suffering. For Dadi, He is a loving Father who, like *any Parent, wants only the best for His children and readily devotes Himself to that. However, He is also the mature and wise Parent who, out of respect for all and the concern to instil a sense of responsibility, will not stand in the way of their making their own choices and so learning from their own mistakes.*

Against this background, here are some of Dadi's insights on God.

God Is Light

God is a point of light, just as we souls are also points of light.

The difference between God and us, is that we take a body. We enter the cycle of physical birth and rebirth and so we begin a slow but gradual state of self-forgetfulness. Over time, the beauty of the human soul becomes tarnished.

God does not take birth in a body. He does not, as do we, gradually lose Himself in a part. For this reason, He is the Supreme Being; He is God, the One who is ever pure.

He is an Ocean of Light, Peace and Love.

Our mind has the ability to take us to the shores of this Ocean.

This is called *yoga.*

God Is Calling Us

It is at this time that God signals to us. It is a silent, almost imperceptible call, but hearing it is the foundation of our spiritual journey.

God is calling us to Himself.

However, we have become so caught up in worldly things that we hardly hear Him.... and yet hear Him we must. The completion of our journey depends on it.

He is signalling us, now, to see and feel ourselves as separate from the body. *"See Me, then see yourself."*

Catching this signal allows us to see the self, the soul, in its original beauty; in its form of divine light. And when we begin to see that self, we are able to see Him, too.

Then there is the realisation that it is His light that is enabling us to see and experience our own.

Recognising Him allows us to recognize ourselves.

And we fall in love with Him for this.

This is also called *yoga*, or making a connection.

God Is the Essence Of All Relationships

The moment has come when the desire to know God is so strong, it enables us to see and recognize Him.

Now is the time to become aware; the time for us to experience His light, love, peace and benevolent power.

When this is experienced, we realise that the essence of all the relationships we have been seeking is now before us.

We understand that our high expectations come from the perfect way we originally experienced every kind of relationship with Him.

He is the true Mother, Father, Friend, Teacher and Guide.

For so long the cry of the heart has been, "Where do I belong? Where do I fit in?"

We looked around the world and felt we belonged nowhere, to no one.

And now here is God, signalling *"You belong with Me. You are Mine."*

To which the soul says, "Yes, I belong here, with You."

And the relationship between the imperishable Supreme Soul and the soul is renewed.

God's help is incognito. It is simply His love. He loves us, as we are and who we are. And as we learn to catch that love, we find our courage and faith increasing, our fears and uncertainties diminishing.

To recognize God as the Father is to understand why God is called the Truth. What is this truth? It is to be a benefactor, to all.

God brings only benefit – not just to one soul, but to all the souls of the world.

God Is Our Mother And Father

God, as the Mother, accepts us exactly as we are.

God does not see our colour, nationality or background, our poverty or our wealth.

God sees only the soul, His child.

No one in the world can accept us so unconditionally. God, as our Mother, doesn't first check us out in any way. The Mother just says, "*Come to Me.*"

The Light says, "*Come to Me. Come into the Light.*"

And then the Mother says, "*Now look at your Father. See who your Father is and what He wants from you.*"

And we see His virtues and powers and know that these are what we want for our life, too. We want His quality of truth.

However, we also know how hard it is to live truthfully in a world like ours.

So the Father says, "*Don't be afraid. Have yoga with Me and I will give you all the strength you need. Link your intellect to Me and I will give you power.*"

God the Father gives another signal to us, "*Child, claim your inheritance.*

You are the imperishable soul and I am your imperishable Father.

You are My child. I give you purity, peace, happiness and love as an inheritance."

And then the Father asks, "*Child, have you received your inheritance? Are you looking after it well?*"

When we recognize the self as a child of God, it becomes easier to let go of old habits.

Pure pride, born of the experience of our divinity, becomes the driving force of our transformation.

God Is Our Teacher

It is a law of the universe that if we love someone we will enjoy listening to them.

God, as the Teacher, has so much to teach us. He introduces us to ourselves. He shows us how to see.

His elevated teachings make our intellect divine. We start to grow cautious about how we use our mind; we no longer wish it to be ordinary. The mind becomes clean, alert, and happy. It ceases to think so much because it is peaceful. If there is a need to think, it does so perfectly, producing solutions.

He teaches us with a lot of patience and love. He does not stop giving. He never tires of this.

Listening to Him, we become sensible. And wise.

God Is Our Guide

God's task, as the Guide, is to watch over us, to stand back and watch us as we learn to live again.

Sometimes He is ahead, clearing the way. At other times, He is not to be seen; He is silently encouraging us from behind.

The Guide ensures that we move in the right direction. And we are freed of any doubts about whether or not we can make this journey.

God Is Our Friend

As a child grows she needs a friend. In addition to her parents, she needs good company. And so God, the Friend, says, "*I will be your Companion. Whatever comes into your heart, tell Me. I will help.*"

God, the Friend, says, "*Keep your heart light*".

And the heart says, "Yes, I want to stay with You, be with You. I want to go home with You."

Worries finish. We feel that everything that was, is and will be, is for the good. Everything becomes good. We eat the nourishment of happiness and become strong.

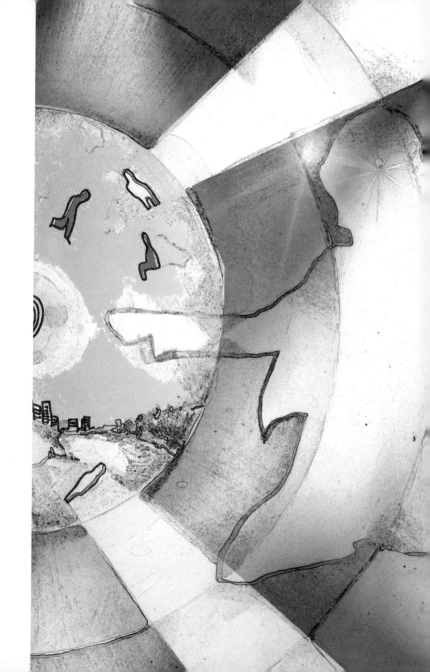

THREE

TOOLS FOR TRANSFORMATION

Understanding our true spiritual nature and connecting with God is the foundation of personal growth, development and change. Without this knowledge and understanding, changes in the self often prove short-lived.

However, knowledge itself is not sufficient. It needs to be put into practice and experienced. Otherwise, it just becomes another interesting set of ideas on the bookshelf of life, something to debate and discuss with others, rather than a way of being. A bit like collecting cookbooks and never baking a cake.

We need to want to transform, and we need to know how to transform.

In this chapter, we explore four interconnected ways of

restoring and developing spiritual greatness: through meditation and yoga, developing our values, using the power of the mind in a positive way and becoming a ruler over our thoughts – a self-sovereign. These experiences of being will inevitably have a profound effect on our lives. Just as a daily programme of physical activity transforms the body, these forms of spiritual workout will improve the mind and spirit.[3]

Meditation and Yoga

Dadi Janki looks at the condition of the soul in the same way that a doctor looks at physical illness. Doctors examine the causes of physical illness in order to find a cure—they check what we have eaten, what we might have picked up from the air, or if we have been resting enough. In the same way, Dadi suggests that we need to check the kind of thoughts we have been feeding our mind, the influences of our surroundings and if we are giving the mind proper rest. The first two factors form the basis of good meditation, which requires the creation of quality thoughts. The third, which involves drawing love from God and cultivating a relationship with the Supreme, is the basis of yoga.

Refresh Yourself

It is not necessary to sit and meditate all day in order to be spiritually sustained. Just as three meals a day provide good nourishment for the body for a full 24 hours, the effects of a good meditation on the soul will also last many hours.

Of course, sitting for some time every day is beneficial – in order to understand certain concepts and to experiment with certain feelings. The idea, however, is to bring these experiences into our life; that is, to allow our feeling of inner well-being to influence our outer world.

In our day-to-day activity, meditation is like a coffee-break for the soul. We simply stop, refresh the mind, then go back to whatever we were doing.

Meditation recharges the battery of the soul. It is a natural way to prevent stress and remain peaceful. It allows us to undertake everything from a feeling of well-being.

Turn Within

We need to take time to sit quietly and observe ourselves objectively.

We should look at our own feelings with a lot of love and say, "Don't worry. Everything will be alright." If we are feeling bad, we need to understand that these bad feelings are not the real me. We need to say to ourselves, "I *am* peace. I *am* love. I *will* regain my original nature. God says it will happen and so it must."

We need to remember that peace is our eternal and original way of life, our original state of being. By turning within and increasing our experience of this, we come to understand and accept that peace is, indeed, our truth.

Let us convince ourselves that peace and happiness can, and surely will, prevail.

Go Into Silence

We all have a sacred space inside us.

In order to experience silence, we must enter this inner world – to think about the self, about God and about the way we should behave.

Discover that peaceful space inside and remain there. Learn to remain silent and peaceful. Even when there is noise and activity around us, this is possible.

God Himself is always in silence. Therefore, to meet Him, we need to go into silence, too.

Think About God

The more we think about the qualities and personality of God, the more we are coloured by His company. Therefore, we need to spend time discovering, contemplating and experiencing the virtues of God.

This is called *yoga*.

There is a lot of power in God's virtues. When we learn how to draw these in, we can change ourselves much more easily than if we try to do it on our own.

A real experience of God enables us to recognize, in a second, everything inside us that is not virtuous.

The light we receive from this experience removes our darkness.

Recharge the Soul

Through the ups and downs of life, the soul has become tired. It needs to find a way to restore itself. But how?

It is only through elevated thinking and a connection with the Supreme that the battery of the soul is recharged. It is as if energy is created.

Most of us are not aware that a feeling of well-being is simply a matter of keeping the inner battery charged.

This is the essence of yoga.

Valuing Our Values

One aspect of transforming ourselves is to recognize and appreciate our inner values. Values are the foundation and decoration of our lives and the key to our motivation. However, a distinction needs to be drawn between the values we acquire from the society in which we happen to live, and those universal values, such as peace and love, which are innate in the soul of every human being.

Many of us might have lost faith in these innate values. In general, we do not seem to be heading towards a kinder, friendlier world and when we look around at our colleagues and friends, it can be seen that many of them have done well even though they have rejected some of these very same values.

Dadi Janki understands that despite their apparent lack of appeal, our inner values are our greatest hope, particularly at this moment in time.

Dadi's faith in values is based on the law of karma, which says that 'as we sow, so we shall reap'; that our 'today' is the result of our 'yesterdays'; that our 'tomorrow' is the result of our 'todays'.[4] This holds all the more significance when we understand the time frame within which Dadi operates. Dadi recognizes that we are at a cusp in the history of humanity; between a 'winter', characterized by a dearth of universal principles and values and a 'spring', in which these same principles and values are in abundance. Dadi believes that now is the time for winter to end and spring to begin.[3] Thus, the values we adopt now are the seeds of the new 'spring'. Therefore, acting from our inner values is a vital feature of world transformation.

In this process, it is not necessary for the whole world population to understand and change, in order for the world to change. The phenomenon of 'critical mass' applies. We need only a critical number of individuals living from their highest values for the mechanism of mass transformation to go into effect.

Here is what Dadi has to say on this topic.

Appreciate Values

Values are possibly the most precious property that we, the human family, possess. They create quality in our lives and relationships and bring dignity to our species. They give life its sparkle.

No one can steal this property, nor can anyone burn it. Values cannot be lost to the soul. They belong to our species, forever.

Values can, however, be neglected. They can get buried under the negative influence of others and the world.

Then, it is as if the soul loses personal meaning. And life loses its soul.

Remove Past Influences

People talk of values but do not often live them. The result of this is artificial beauty.

True beauty is the result of removing all traces of corruption, lies, bias and prejudice from our memory track.

Such things kill the conscience and make us weak. We succumb to outside pressures and do not do what we know we should.

We deceive ourselves.

To deceive oneself is the worst form of deception.

Cultivate Values

Values do not grow easily in a mind filled with negativity.

Such terrain needs to be worked on with hope and the spade of personal accountability, and made fertile through the water of good thoughts and pure feelings. Then our values, like seeds, will grow - from the inside, out.

We need to protect our values from adverse influences. We must neither blame others, nor feel the victim.

Prepare and nurture your values well, and whenever there is an opportunity, share them with love.

The first values we need to encourage in ourselves are honesty and altruism.

Understand the Time

Just as the darkness of night is followed by day, so too this winter for humanity will give way to the blossoms of spring.

When it is the season for planting, a farmer knows he has work to do. His attention goes to what seeds need to be sown. He makes no excuses. He cannot afford to be careless.

In the same way, now is the time to let our values emerge.

It is through them that the value of life is increased.

Do Good

A better life, a better world, is in our own hands and, no one else's.

With pure values we can move a mountain. It is not a big thing. Human beings can do whatever they set their mind to.

Now is the time to give such attention to the soul. The long winter for humanity is coming to an end, and the new spring is about to begin.

This is the season to become good.

The Positive Mind

Understanding the power of the mind, is the first step to taking control of it. Thoughts, which are created through it, are a form of energy[5] *and, like any other form of energy, can be used for the benefit of the self and others, or can be used destructively. The choice is ours.*

Dadi Janki refuses to entertain any negative thoughts about herself, others, or life. She knows that the soul originally was completely free of negativity and so she sees only the best in people and believes that by concentrating on that, they will find the courage and hope to change.

Here are some of Dadi's insights on the power of a positive mind.

Control Your Mind

We think too much.

Many types of thought enter the mind, leaving no space to experience silence for even one second.

We need to examine these thoughts. In what direction are they going? If we keep turning negative thoughts over and over again in the mind, it is like drinking contaminated water.

It will make us sick.

There is no need for our thoughts to go racing about in every direction.

Consider the mind to be like a little baby, and give it love, care and attention. Constantly.

This is what it means to, take charge of the mind.

We *can* give the mind what it needs, what it is looking for.

The first requirement for this is to make time for quiet reflection.

Unite Your Heart and Mind

Sit quietly and let your mind and heart start talking to each other.

Notice how discouraged the mind has become.

The mind will say, "I am so exhausted and confused I can hardly hear you. All I want is some rest."

The racing mind is really only looking for joy – the

internal, spiritual happiness that is independent of the physical senses.   Because the mind is distanced from this spiritual experience, it has lost true happiness.

The mind has got into a rut, caused by the habit of over- thinking the 'how', 'why' and 'but' of every situation. Thinking of that which is good has become a struggle. Often, negativity fills the mind, in regard to both the self and others, emptying it of its value and beauty.

Notice, also, how unhappy the heart has become.

The heart says, "I have never found what I really wanted. I'm not happy being driven by desires."

Has anyone ever understood that pain in our heart? Even when we tried to touch and explain it, was anyone really able to hear us?

No one was even listening. So these things were left inside, layering the heart in sorrow and pain.

When the mind and heart don't understand each other, the result is depression.

Depression is very common these days.

Learn to Love Yourself

The key to positive, constructive thinking is true love for oneself.

What is true self love?

To experience this, we need to catch the love that God is sharing with us. The experience of love, coming from God, *is* the experience of self love.

We have to open ourselves to this pure love coming to us from God. This love is the true comfort that the heart and mind have been seeking.

Be Aware of Negative Feelings

Many on a spiritual path are wary of negative thoughts and feelings, and so, when they come up, they often try to suppress them. They force themselves not to think about what has happened, or carry on as if everything is all right.

However, to move along in this way is to be deceived.

Simply suppressing negativity does not work. More and more people understand this, and they no longer want to suppress their emotions. Indeed, suppression has become something to be feared.

However, it is not the suppression of our negativity that is the most frightening, but the suppression of our innate capacity for greatness.

Often, our own negativity can be so pervasive and subtle that we do not even realise that it is suppressing a whole world of inner, divine goodness.

We need to open ourselves to that internal world of goodness.

The power of our inner greatness will work to remove the fears.

All this needs to be understood if we want to overcome our habit of suppression.

Allow Pure Feelings to Emerge

We transform through allowing ourselves to acknowledge the original, divine feelings of the soul. When we justify our own negativity, defend it, or allow ourselves to act from negative patterns, we suppress these pure feelings.

Keep guard over whatever is going on inside you and respond with words, or actions, based on peace and love.

When qualities are born of a genuine relationship between the highest form of ourselves and with God, negativity truly finishes.

End Subservience

The reason it is difficult to remain constantly happy is that the soul has become a slave to negative ways of thinking and behaving.

Originally the master, the soul has now become a slave to these bad habits .

Some say they want to change, but often, the desire to change is not real. Old habits serve us; we get something from them.

This is a very subtle reason for much of our loss of happiness and power.

Look at Yourself, Not at Others

We avoid the responsibility of doing the real work needed to change things in ourselves by looking at others. We become lawyers and judges. Because of this external focus, our own well-being fluctuates. One moment we blossom, the next we wilt.

However, the crux of a spiritual education is to understand who *we* are, and what it is that *we* could be doing. This is what we need to preoccupy ourselves with. We do not have the right to make the ways of others our concern.

Explain these things to yourself, rather than to others.

This is a good first step towards change.

We need to think about what *we* have to do. And do it. not later but now.

Let Go

We will only be free of our old patterns when we let go of them. They are not going to let go of us. We have to let go of them.

By thinking of the past, the present can become weak.

The past belongs to the past. We must let go of it, because it does not belong to us. If we hold on to things that are not useful, we cannot change.

We must realize our mistakes, have the determined thought not to repeat them and move on. This is the basis of 'letting go'.

Do It Now

We need to change. But when will we change? Today? Tomorrow? Next year?

We need to change *now*.

If not now, then when?

Abolish words like, 'try'. If we say, "We will try it", when will we try? There is power in saying, "Yes!" and changing something in ourselves straight away.

If not you, then who?

Self Sovereignty

Once we understand the power of thoughts, we can begin to take control of our lives – to gather up the reins that we so often put into the hands of others.

Meditation allows us to start making decisions based on the truth of who we really are, rather than on the opinions of our friends or society. We become less and less ruled by our negative patterns and emotions, which in turn helps us to develop true love and respect for the self. Courage is restored – the courage to break old habits, stop making excuses, to see our own greatness and to live according to that vision. We become rulers of the self. There is self-mastery.

For those who wish to become self-sovereigns, Dadi makes the following suggestions:

Realise the True Self

Trying to change ourselves through force is not necessary. The truth of who we are holds the power to create all the changes we desire.[6]

We simply need to realize, believe and accept the highest truth about ourselves.

Developing this faith is our primary spiritual responsibility. It is the foundation of all other efforts. It is easy to construct the part of the building that is above ground. The real work lies in creating the foundation.

Spiritual determination means to be motivated by a taste of inner well-being. It means to be inspired by happiness rather than shaped by sorrow.

Self-realization leads to self-transformation.

See No Evil

People may have defects but we are the owners of our eyes and so it is up to us to choose what we see. If we focus on the shortcomings of others, those shortcomings will become ours.

Remember, everyone has a special quality; everyone is unique and is playing their own part. Let us focus on their uniqueness and specialities.

Keep Cool

The more angry a person is, the weaker that person becomes.

In front of such a person, be merciful. Maintain your dignity and that will enable them to regain theirs.

Be Independent

To depend on others makes us weak and insecure. Seeking the love and approval of others, we become trapped in a deceptive game of give and take: "I will love you, if you will love me."

It is better to give rather than take. It is better to be 'in-dependent' : to turn '*inward*' and '*depend*' on the self.

Keep Good Company

Two types of friendship commonly exist. One gives nurture and support; and one is based on gossip and selfishness.

What everyone needs now are friends that support them spiritually.

Develop Pure Pride

The ability to master our emotions is based on pure pride.

Pure pride is not ego.

Identifying too strongly with the roles we play leads to ego and we become affected by the opinions of others, such as praise or defamation.

Ego hardens the heart.

Pure pride is the result of exploring our spiritual heritage. It is based on the awareness of being a soul and a child of God.

The flame of pure pride is re-ignited by the experience of peace and love flowing from the heart. It is the basis of elevated, unshakeable self-respect. It makes us self-sovereigns and naturally generous-hearted.

When we operate from pure pride, we are not distressed by the negativity of others. Our peace of mind remains intact, even in the face of insult.

Keep Giving

Sins are mistakes and, actions performed while separated from the experience of one's true self and God.

Consequently, we feel empty and use people and things to satisfy ourselves. This makes us into 'takers', beggars of life, always looking for ways to get more for ourselves.

The opposite of sin is spiritual charity; pure altruism.

When the soul remembers its truth and forges a connection with the Supreme, it flows like a river and becomes a tireless, unconditional server.

This spiritual charity transforms us from beggars into kings, the true children of God.

Help Others Through Love

Souls can only change when surrounded by love. To think of trying to change others – not to mention oneself – without love, is like trying to move a car without turning on the engine. Give love and regard to one another. Be more sensitive to the power of words, which can either be like a knife to the heart - killing it; or a needle and thread - mending it.

We have to have a big heart. Let go of the habit of entertaining unnecessary thoughts about others. Criticism, jealousy and ego are companions which support each other, weakening the true self and damaging others.

Be Non-Violent

There is a deep connection between non-violence and truth. They have a strong friendship with each other; it is as though they are brothers. Where one is present, the other is there, too. If we are not able to feel love for ourselves, family or friends, it means there is some kind of violence inside ourselves.

Any type of negative thought is in fact violence. Anger, for instance, often begins with thoughts such as, 'I do not like this'.

Being hard on ourselves, rather than making self-effort with love, patience and faith, is also violence.

So is rejecting others. People don't have time to listen with love, yet they have the time to speak harsh words.

To put someone down, to make another person fall, to be uncaring about others, are all forms of violence. People have a heart, but it is as if many are heartless. There is no mercy, or compassion.

Only when there is Godly truth in the heart can there be true, Godly love to share with others.

Explore Godly Virtue

There is a difference between human virtue and Godly virtue. Human virtue always demands some recognition of its goodness, on one level or another. It seeks praise.

Godly virtue does not. It has been awakened by God and filled with God's strength. The sign of Godly virtue is that it does not seek to control.

Seeking to control others disempowers them.

It also disempowers the self.

FOUR

CLEARING UP THE MESS

The current state of the world is the collective result of the individual thoughts, words, actions and consciousness of each of us. Thus, world poverty is the result of a poverty of spiritual values, including our lack of compassion and care for our fellow brothers and sisters. Violence, in its various forms, comes from the frustration and anger felt by individuals who have lost respect for themselves and others. Global pollution is a reflection of a disrespect for nature and a form of mental pollution and arrogance, which has blinded us to the intimate connection between nature and ourselves.

For Dadi Janki, the task of clearing up this mess is a joint responsibility between ourselves and God. God, as an incorporeal Being, cannot do the job without our cooperation and we cannot do it without His knowledge and power. And so we become His instruments for world transformation and renewal.

With great compassion and unrelenting optimism, Dadi connects all those she meets to their latent greatness and inspires them to strengthen their faith in, and commitment to, a higher state of goodness. She knows from her own experience that great things can be achieved with love, faith, power and understanding. Change the hearts and minds of human beings and you will automatically change the world.

In the following insights, Dadi shows us how to avail ourselves of God's support and encourages us to join her on the world stage and play our part in helping God to transform the world. In so doing, we restore our spiritual greatness.

The Task

The task of world change is God's task, but He gets this done through the virtuous acts of humans. The basis of this is pure spiritual love, from the heart.

Many people are afraid of the word 'spirituality'. They are even afraid of the word 'love'. However, both these terms simply offer an understanding of what it means to be a true, indeed a great, human being.

These unique times herald a new day; they are the final storms before the spring, at long last, arrives.[7]

Therefore, do whatever you need to do but do it with clarity, wisdom and love.[8] These are the spiritual seeds that will create the garden of the new spring, and bring the long winter of humanity to an end.

Recognise Your Spiritual Power

The intention of good spiritual practice is to change ourselves and through this, to change the world. As we change, the world changes.

Many people, however, are cynical about this. They wonder how, or when, people will change. This is understandable.

For many, a life of peace and love has been replaced by such fast living that often people don't even have the time to greet each other properly, let alone smile. Instead, there is only worry. "I don't have the time. I can't be bothered…".

These are the excuses of our times.

We have forgotten the reality of our higher truth and no longer understand that there is power in actions that are shaped by elevated consciousness. We do not realise how important this time is.[9]

Use Your Spiritual Power

A spiritual life-style does not require that we leave our family, or profession.

On the contrary, we use our spirituality and serve *through* our responsibilities in the world.

Spirituality is simply a way of seeing everything clearly and, therefore, removing difficulties.

Never Betray the Self

When the oil in a car runs low, the engine starts to overheat. In the same way, when the 'oil' of our original, pure and positive feelings begins to run low, it is easy to overheat with stress and anger as we move along life's journey.

In one second we can become irritated and annoyed and lose our inner peace and power.

When this is the state of the soul over a long period of time, the heart becomes layered with feelings of depression, guilt and fear. The mind begins to lose its strength of conviction and the idea of leading a life of wisdom and truth seems too idealistic.

Spiritual dishonesty creeps into the soul and we convince ourselves that it is old-fashioned to have values. We say, "How can we survive in today's world if we continue to be honest, loving, or humble?" We cease to listen to our inner voice and doubts emerge about the value of our higher truths. This is a kind of self-betrayal, which causes the soul to stop trusting itself and others.

Strengthen the Heart Through Experience

To step forward, to be an individual, who pioneers change at the roots, we have to break the cycle of self-deception and mistrust. How?

It is a matter of creating balance between the heart and the head.

In recent times, we have developed the habit of thinking too much. This has tired the mind, causing it to become weak and easily influenced.

We need to tune in to the original, divine feelings deep within the heart. They are truly there; we just have to emerge them.

When such feelings are again *experienced* by the heart, and not just simply understood by the head, our values begin to clarify and reaffirm themselves, automatically. We are able to discern right from wrong and actually *do* what is right. We become free from external influences and behave in a way that reflects the higher self.

In this way, the mind is strengthened and begins to create right thoughts.

When the feelings in the heart are true, then, whatever the mind thinks will be right.

The need is removed to think so much.

Help Divine Feelings to Emerge

Let divine feelings that are deep inside the heart emerge.

This will make everything else easy. It is easier to think of them emerging than transforming.[10] Less effort is required.

When true feelings of peace are allowed once again to emerge in the heart, there will be feelings of love, too. This, in turn, will bring power. Where there is inner peace, there is always love and strength.

Such things have nothing to do with religion, or culture. In any situation, anywhere in the world, if there is peace and love, life *will* change. Relationships *will* improve. Inner peace and love generate a spiritual energy that allows us to be of true service to the world.

Be a Channel for God's Energy

The original source of divine energies and, therefore, divine experiences, is God.

By keeping ourselves in His company, we can draw from His peace and love, so that it is His energy that does the work. There is no need to use our own energy. Trying to do it on our own will only exhaust us.

We become His instruments and let *Him* do it *through* us. In this way, everything can be accomplished, easily.

When we act as instruments, miracles begin to happen.

Problems and difficulties change. Everything gets done, leaving us with the feeling of having done nothing. We feel completely light – indeed, we *are* filled with His light and people notice. They will pick up our vibrations of peace and love and begin to smile. There will be little need for idle chit chat.

They will want to know how we got this way.

Whoever we are in contact with will be touched by God. Such is the spiritual power available to us now.

But first, we have to make ourselves peaceful and loving.

Become Peaceful

Being peaceful takes practise.

The ability to centre ourselves in peace is the first and most important step in serving others.

Learn to be quiet.

Explore the connection between peace and love. This combination enables hearts to be healed. Peace alone is not enough. It is peace plus God's love that heals hearts. Prove this to yourself.

Let there be stillness within. Experience the exquisite and subtle connection with God. Bathe in His many qualities. Become quiet, peaceful and clear.

Through deep silence, the mind creates right thoughts and words. Naturally, easily, without thinking too much, we are able to refresh others by our company.

Become a Lighthouse

A lighthouse signals where ships should or should not go; it shows where safety lies. This is how we can help serve the world now. We must show others the way, through our own elevated actions and behaviour.

Be like the sun and serve the whole world.

Go beyond the thought, "I am doing it" or "I have to do it'" The dynamic of true charity is this: our elevated state of being *allows* everything to get done. By Him.

This is how to be of true service to others.

Believe in Others

We must never give up on people, or lose hope.

People may give up on themselves, others may give up on them too, but those of us who want to help in world renewal must never give up on others.

Some may condemn a person, or wonder why we continue to bother with someone who is not showing any signs of change. They feel our time would be better spent on someone more promising.

However, in a hospital, would doctors not give oxygen to a dying patient right up to the end? There is no question of leaving them and moving on to another one. What would that be called?

When we have truly experienced the unshakeable faith that God has in us, it becomes our duty to believe in others and offer that same kind of support.

This is the duty of the true server and helper of others: to care, share and inspire, unconditionally.

PARTING WORD

We hope you have enjoyed reading this handbook and that it will become a source of inspiration and guidance in your journey of self-discovery and change.

Restoring the greatness of our spirit and playing our part in creating heaven on earth is both a noble vision and a mission that gives us the clarity and courage to face the future with confidence and hope and make the most of our life in these challenging times. If you would like to know more about the philosophy of the Brahma Kumaris as exemplified in the talks by Dadi Janki, please contact your local Brahma Kumaris Meditation Centre.

MORE FOOD FOR THOUGHT

1. The Powerful Mind

The power of the human mind is the greatest power we possess. Thoughts created through it manifest themselves in words and actions, which affect not only the self and others but, ultimately, the world as well. The world is, therefore, a reflection of our consciousness.

Everything created by human beings is first created in the mind, through thoughts. Our hopes, dreams, visions, our attitudes and values, our awareness and ways of seeing the world, all spring from the seed of our thoughts. Through our thoughts we create our destiny. For example, the thoughts of Edison led to the creation of electricity, which has significantly contributed to an improved standard of living for all. The thoughts of Gandhi led to the liberation of a whole nation through non-violent resistance. This provided a long-lasting global inspiration for the resolution of conflict through peaceful means.

Thoughts may be divided into five types, namely:

necessary thoughts, which are useful to life, such as "I must buy some food now."

wasteful thoughts, which are non-productive, such as endlessly dreaming of winning a lottery, or mindlessly going over and over something from the past.

negative thoughts, which damage the self and others, such as "I don't like you."

positive thoughts, which bring benefit to the self and others, such as "I'm sure she is trying her best."

elevated thoughts, which, based on spiritual knowledge, reinforce the link between ourselves and God, such as "I am a peaceful soul."

If we wish to change ourselves it is obvious that we need to create positive thoughts about ourselves and others. Often, this is a challenge, because over the years we have been greatly affected by the negative thoughts of others, such as our parents, teachers and employers. Consequently, many of us do not feel good about ourselves. We suffer from low self-esteem and a lack of self-respect, which can leave us feeling crippled inside.

We need to check and change such thoughts, replacing them with the elevated thoughts and the power of deep love that comes from knowing our true spiritual self and God.

2. We Reap What We Sow

Turning inwards, developing higher levels of consciousness, experiencing the Divine – all these have little value if they are not used to create concrete positive changes in our personal well-being, in our relationships and in our ability to play our roles responsibly in the world.

The need to bring spirituality into our daily living becomes particularly clear when we understand the law of cause and effect. This law states that there is no such thing as a coincidence, that whatever is happening is the result ('effect') of something that happened in the past (the 'cause').

On the spiritual path, this is known as the law of karma. In essence, this law is telling us that whatever comes in front of us today, is a result of our yesterdays.

It is the spiritual equivalent of what is more commonly known as Newton's 'Third Law of Motion', which states that 'for every action there is an equal and opposite reaction'. We also say, "Your past always catches up with you", "Everything that comes around, goes around," or, "As you sow, so you shall reap".

However, this does not mean that our life needs to be forever controlled by choices we have made in the past, and that there is nothing we can do about it.

On the contrary, this law is an invitation to personal creativity, responsibility and ultimate accountability. I can take the law back into my own hands, here and now. How?

By realizing that this same law also states that whatever is our tomorrow will be the result of our actions today.

The law of karma draws our attention to the importance of the present. Everything we do today is like a seed sown in the garden of our life. If the seed is of good quality, so will be its fruit. The quality of our 'garden' (i.e. our life) depends on the seeds we sow. Today. It is in our hands.

Here we see the value of spiritual awareness.

Experiencing the self as a soul and remaining linked to the Supreme Soul is the easy way to stay filled with the positive qualities needed to grow a beautiful, healthy garden of life. Genuine feelings of joy and peace create a far better quality 'seed' than feelings of anger, or resentment.

When we respond to the events of life by drawing on the experience of our spiritual self-realisation, we will be the master of our destiny. When we react to life on the basis of ego, anger, greed or the many other characteristics that are less than divine, we remain a slave to the circumstances and situations of life, with not much hope for change. The choice – to respond responsibly, or react unthinkingly – will always be ours.

Spiritual practice enables us to become the best we can be. Thinking, feeling and performing to the best of our ability creates a better life for ourselves and, therefore, the world.

3. New Perspectives on Time

The concept of time being linear, i.e. having a definite beginning and an ultimate end, is not a universally accepted idea.

Many people, especially in the East, believe time to be cyclical; i.e. it has its own natural repeating rhythm of expansion and contraction, growth and decay. There is considerable evidence, especially in the world of nature, to support this view. For example, the cycle of the seasons (spring, summer, autumn and winter), of plants, of day and night and the tides.

In some Eastern traditions, there is an understanding that the history and geography of the world can be viewed in terms of four ages, or stages, namely: the golden, silver, copper and iron ages. The 'golden age' represents a time when the souls of the earth are completely pure, peaceful and positive, living in complete harmony, in a world of abundance and beauty. Then a gradual decline occurs leading to the 'iron age', which reflects the final degraded state of both souls and nature, when spiritual and physical energies are at their lowest.

Between the end of the 'iron age' and the beginning of the 'golden age', there is a transitional stage, known as the 'confluence age'. At this time, human beings remember their true spiritual identity and make efforts to return to their original state of pure energy with the help of the Supreme Being. Because the outer physical world is a reflection of the state of our inner, spiritual world, this change of consciousness, and the related changes in our character and behaviour, trigger the start of a new golden age.

The cyclical way of understanding time, nature and our own history may be controversial but it is both empowering and reassuring compared with the linear model, which offers no light at the end of the tunnel.

4. Inner Qualities

We *are* divine beings, even though we may no longer be accustomed to thinking of ourselves in this way.

The purpose of good spiritual practice is to allow this divinity to re-emerge within our personality. When we think that we are simply bringing out something that is already there, rather than forcing ourselves to adopt new behaviours, the process of self-transformation becomes easier.

Here are just some of our many original qualities, written in the form of affirmations.

1. ACCEPTANCE...I recognize and embrace the benefit in every moment and the beauty in every soul

2. ACCURACY...My care, consideration and attention inspires enthusiasm, confidence and trust in all around me

3. CAREFREE... I accept responsibility without burden and face the future without fear

4. COMPASSION...I keep a firm, clear vision of each one's goodness and specialities and help restore their self-belief

5. CONTENTMENT... I remain unaffected in the midst of constant change, maintaining awareness of all my other virtues

6. DETERMINATION...I have faith in my ability to change and the courage to make those changes is reflected in all my actions

7. ENTHUSIASM...My appreciation and love for all that comes my way, breathes life into every situation

8. FREEDOM... I am unaffected and unburdened by the past or future and so I am free to experience the true essence of my own being, now

9. GENEROSITY... I share with others all that I value in myself, with open hands and an open heart

10. GENTLENESS...I reach out to the world from a place of quietness and trust...offering gifts of kindness and comfort without touching, or disturbing

11. HAPPINESS... I easily see life's beauty, hear her song and dance to her music because I am deeply content with who I am

12. HONESTY...I am true to the best that is in me and I willingly let go of anything less

13. HOPE...I open the window to a bright future by firmly closing the door on the past

14. HUMILITY...I reflect the quiet knowledge of my own value and the equal value of others in my every thought and action

15. INTROVERSION... I enjoy touching the stillness and pure love that lie at the centre of my being

16. LIGHTNESS...I remain inside the happiness of the present moment and so I am free from past burdens, or future concerns

17. PATIENCE... I am willing to let time and life move forward at their right pace, without losing sight of my destination

18. POSITIVE...I am alert to the deeper meaning in every situation and enjoy every lesson that life offers me

19. PURITY... I stand in the sacred place within me and allow the light of truth to wash me clean

20. SELF RESPECT... I embrace the journey toward my full potential, appreciating my qualities and encouraging inner change

21. SIMPLICITY... I approach the complications of life with a clear and balanced mind that is free from desire

22. STRENGTH... I support and protect myself and others, by believing in myself and the quiet, insistent force that lies within me

23. TOLERANCE... I appreciate the richness that different opinions and perspectives bring to the tapestry of life and so remain calm and contented

24. TRUST... I step forward into life with confidence, knowing the fullness of who I am and the inherent goodness of others

25. WISDOM...I am guided by the richness of experience folded inside me and by a quiet appreciation of life's lessons

5. The Eight Powers

When we begin to explore our spiritual identity, eight forms of power become available to us. Being aware of these powers is especially useful in times of difficulty, when we need to maintain our inner strength and resourcefulness.

The first power – called the power to **withdraw** – is the ability to transform useless thought patterns into a higher state of awareness. It allows us to 'withdraw' from negativity – inner as well as outer – enabling us to respond and not merely react to the people and situations that surround us.

The second power is much like the first, but more related to emotions and feelings. With this power – called the power to **merge** – we can easily see the less than divine feelings still harboured within the heart. We learn to allow those unworthy feelings to be dissolved by God's light and love. This transforms them, leaving us with feelings of compassion, no matter what the situation, or behaviour of others.

When these first two powers begin working for us, our head and heart become healthier. This is the basis for the next two powers, the powers to tolerate and accommodate.

When **tolerance** begins to operate as a power, it is the people around us who notice. We, ourselves, are hardly aware of it. An image used for this power is a fruit-laden tree, yielding its fruits to children who are throwing stones in an attempt to shake the fruits free. Tolerance as a power works in the same way. We are not affected by the stones being thrown at us. We remain untroubled and, effortlessly, continue to give of our 'fruits' – the healthy thoughts and feelings that come from our innate goodness.

A river rarely moves in a hard straight line from its start to its end. A river weaves and flows; it accommodates the twists and turn of the land, yet it does so without ever losing its direction, always pulled toward its ultimate destination. In the same way, the power to **accommodate** – the fourth power

– allows us to flow with life, to take in our stride its many twists and turns, without ever losing our focus, or compromising our aim.

The fifth power of **discernment** is the ability to know clearly the difference between right and wrong. However, '*knowing*' alone does not always empower. Therefore, to act according to that knowledge is the sixth power – to **judge** – which gives us the ability and strength to translate an enlightened consciousness into elevated, yet practical, action

The power to **face** enables us to direct the light of our truth into the last dark corners of the soul. We find ourselves easily able to face down the last of our short-comings which, in turn, enables us to handle the difficult situations in our daily life responsibly. As the light grows, the darkness is vanquished.

The eighth power – to **cooperate** – calls on all the other seven to enable the soul to serve at all times – selflessly, generously and tirelessly. This is actually what spiritual power is all about: the ability to sustain virtue and goodness in all situations and to help others do so, too. It is not about self transformation alone; it's about the world transformation that will take place when enough of us start to live from our highest truth, together in unity and harmony.

6. Lifestyle Matters

The process of transformation outlined by Dadi Janki, i.e. reconnecting with the inner being and God and changing the way we relate to others, provides a firm foundation for restoring our greatness and goodness.

However, it is not sufficient in itself. Changes in consciousness need to be reinforced by a number of practical life style changes, if they are to have maximum impact.

The following are some of the practices recommended by the Brahma Kumaris for supplementing spiritual endeavour.

Daily Meditation: the most powerful time to meet with the Supreme Being is in the early morning hours, before the activities of the world begin. Meditation at this time enables the soul to be charged for the day

Periodic breaks of a few minutes throughout the day, as well as half an hour each evening at 7:00pm, help to restore the energies of the soul during, and after, the challenges of the day

Regular Spiritual Study: just as the body needs nourishment, so does the soul. A daily input of empowering, inspirational, spiritual teachings keeps the mind usefully occupied and provides insights for meditation and guidance for our behaviour

Wholesome Diet: the food, drink and other substances we take into the body not only affect our physical health but also our state of mind. Meditation requires a stable, calm mind free from such mind-altering substances as alcohol, tobacco, drugs and other stimulants. Vegetarian food, made with love and offered to God, has a powerful positive impact on both the soul and the body and more than compensates for any feeling of loss we might experience, initially, when changing other aspects of our diet.

Good Company: following a spiritual path is made easier if we associate with like-minded people, who share similar values and aspirations

Wholesome Mind: the subconscious mind is like a tape recorder. It records whatever it picks up and then replays it. In other words, when we take in rubbish, that is what we will give out. So, we need to protect ourselves from such soul- destroying activities as gossiping, and books and films of a vicious and/or violent nature. Such activities disturb our peace of mind.

Serve Others: being positive and co-operative in our relationships with others is the bedrock on which we develop our spiritual skills, virtues and qualities. The world is a mirror for the state of our consciousness and a laboratory in which we can experiment and grow in strength and goodness.

These are just some of the more important ways in which we can develop a spiritual lifestyle. Following these practices can be quite challenging, especially as there are huge influences in the form of the media and peer pressure, which we have to face and overcome. However, these challenges are designed to make us strong. Choosing to be good and become great in these circumstances, is not for the faint-hearted, but it brings a lot of satisfaction!

7. Walking the Talk

The Brahma Kumaris was founded in 1936 by Dada Lekhraj, a wealthy, philanthropic, diamond merchant and head of a large family, who lived at the time in Sindh (now part of Pakistan). Having reached the age of 60, Dada was preparing to retire from his business when he had a series of profound revelations relating to the future of the world and the role he would play in it.

Soon afterwards, he became an instrument for the channelling of powerful, spiritual knowledge and it was not long before a community of about 300 people, mainly women, grew up around him.

Brahma Baba, as he became known, used his considerable financial resources to support this community. With great foresight and courage, at a time when women in

India were usually considered third class citizens at best, he appointed a group of eight young women to manage its affairs. He became a practical and inspiring example of how the power of spirituality can restore humanity to its original divine state. His teachings, humility, respect and genuine care for others, created an environment in which everyone could learn and grow and fulfil their innate potential.

For nearly 13 years, Brahma Baba and the community lived in self-imposed isolation, developing a deep understanding of the self, practising what is now known as Brahma Kumaris Raja Yoga meditation, and creating a spiritual family based on love and service.

In the early 1950's, the community moved to its current headquarters in Mt. Abu, in the state of Rajasthan, where it continued to grow slowly and surely. Soon afterwards, the young women, who had now become teachers in their own right, were sent in pairs to different parts of India to establish new centres under the guidance of Brahma Baba, who eventually died in 1969 at the age of 93.

Service started outside India in the early 1970's. There are now over 8,000 centres in more than 90 countries.

In 1996, the University's Academy for a Better World was opened in Mount Abu, India. The Academy offers individuals, from all walks of life, opportunities for life-long innovative learning. Residential programmes are centred on human, moral and spiritual values and principles. The University also supports the Global Hospital and Research Centre in Mount Abu.

Some of the key features of the Brahma Kumaris are:

it is female-led. Although men make an important contribution to the organization, it is recognized that women have a special role to play in helping to heal the world at this critical time. Also, as the soul is genderless, both men and women are encouraged to develop all aspects of themselves so that their relationships can become more equal and balanced.

all its activities are offered free of charge. The Brahma Kumaris believe that spiritual knowledge, like air and water, should be freely available to all. The organization is funded by the donations of its students and well-wishers.

it operates on the understanding that the world will change only when we change. It offers, free of charge, a wide range of courses, seminars and retreats to facilitate this process – including positive thinking, Raja Yoga meditation, self-esteem, and stress and anger management.

it actively engages with the world. It is affiliated to the United Nations as a non-governmental organization in general consultative status with the UN Economic and Social Council and in consultative status with UNICEF. It also works jointly with all types of organizations in many different areas of life such as education, health, social welfare, the business community and inter-faith movement.

In India, the Brahma Kumaris are well established and highly regarded at all levels of society and in 1992 a national stamp was issued to commemorate Brahma Baba's contribution to humanity.

NOTES

[1] See More Food for Thought 7: Walking the Talk: About the Brahma Kumaris

[2] Please note that God, like all other souls, is a Being of qualities and as such, does not have a gender. The term 'He' is used for convenience.

[3] See More Food for Thought 6: Lifestyle Matters

[4] See More Food for Thought 2: We Reap What We Sow

[5] See More Food for Thought 1: The Powerful Mind

[6] See More Food for Thought 4: Inner Qualities

[7] See More Food for Thought 3: New Perspectives on Time

[8] See More Food for Thought 5: The Eight Powers

[9] See More Food for Thought 3: New Perspectives on Time

[10] See More Food for Thought 4: Inner Qualities

Other books to feed the soul

If you have enjoyed reading this book on Raja Yoga meditation as taught by the Brahma Kumaris World Spiritual University, you might like to read the following books to enhance your meditation practice and deepen your spiritual understanding.

All the above books and a variety of meditation commentaries and meditation music are available from
www.bkpublications.com

About the Brahma Kumaris World Spiritual University

The Brahma Kumaris World Spiritual University is an international organisation working at all levels of society for positive change. Established in 1937, the University now has over 8,000 centres in more than 90 countries. It actively participates in a wide range of educational programmes in areas such as youth, women, men, environment, peace, values, social development, education, health and human rights.

In 1996, the University's Academy for a Better World was opened in Mount Abu, India. The Academy offers individuals from all walks of life opportunities for life-long innovative learning. Residential programmes are centred on human, moral and spiritual values and principles. The University also supports the Global Hospital and Research Centre in Mount. Abu , India.

Local centres around the world provide courses and lectures in meditation and positive values, supporting individuals in recognising their own inherent qualities and abilities, and making the most of their lives.

All courses and activities are offered free of charge.

International Headquarters
Po Box No 2, Mount Abu 307501,
Rajasthan, India.
Tel: (+91) 2974-38261 to 68
Fax: (+91) 2974-38952
E-mail: abu@bkindia.com

International Co-Ordinating Office &
Regional Office For Europe And The Middle East
Global Co-operation House,
65-69 Pound Lane, London, NW10 2HH, UK
Tel: (+44) 208 727 3350
Fax: (+44) 208 727 3351
E-mail: london@bkwsu.com

REGIONAL OFFICES

Africa
Global Museum for a Better World,
Maua Close, off Parklands Road, Westlands,
PO Box 123, Sarit Centre, Nairobi, Kenya
Tel: (+254) 20-374 3572
Fax: (+254) 20-374 3885
E-mail: bkwsugm@holidaybazaar.com

Australia And South East Asia
78 Alt Street, Ashfield, Sydney, NSW 2131, Australia
Tel: (+61) 2 9716 7066
Fax: (+61) 2 9716 7795
E-mail: indra@brahmakumaris.com.au

The Americas And The Caribbean
Global Harmony House, 46 S. Middle Neck Road,
Great Neck, NY 11021, USA
Tel: (+1) 516 773 0971
Fax: (+1) 516 773 0976
E-mail: newyork@bkwsu.com

Russia, Cis And The Baltic Countries
2 Gospitalnaya Ploschad, Build. 1
Moscow - 111020, Russia
Tel: (+7) 095 263 02 47
Fax: (+7) 095 261 32 24
E-mail: bkwsu@mail.ru

http://www.bkwsu.org

Brahma Kumaris Publications
www.bkpublications.com
enquiries@bkpublications.com